LIONS

EYE TO EYE WITH BIG CATS

Jason Cooper

Rourke

Publishing LLC

Vero Beach, Florida 32964

www.rourkepublishing.com

PHOTO CREDITS: All photos © Lynn M. Stone

Cover Photo: *Although they are nearly extinct in Asia, lions are still common on the grasslands of Africa.*

Editor: Frank Sloan

Cover design by Nicola Stratford

Library of Congress Cataloging-in-Publication Data

Cooper, Jason, 1942-
 Lions / Jason Cooper.
     p. cm. — (Eye to eye with big cats)
Includes bibliographical references (p.   ).
 ISBN 1-58952-405-5 (hardcover)
 1. Lions—Juvenile literature. [1. Lions. 2. Endangered species.] I.
Title.

 QL737.C23 C6747 2002
 599.757—dc21

                                                    2002003654

Printed in the USA

CG/CG

TABLE OF CONTENTS

THE LION

The lion (*Panthera leo*) is one of the world's most powerful creatures. It is one of the biggest cats. Only the tiger is larger.

As well as being big, the lion is loud. It has a big voice and a mighty roar. Because of these, the lion is sometimes called the "king of the beasts."

A female lion hunts in the tall grass of the East African plain.   5

THE LION'S RELATIVES

The lion is related to all cats, known as **felines**. These big cats include jaguars, leopards, and tigers. Like all these cats, the lion is a **carnivore**, or meat-eater.

Like the other cats, the lion has short jaws, sharp claws and teeth, and a long, flexible body. There is just one **species**, or kind, of lion. There are some differences among lions, though.

The lion of India does not have a thick mane like the African lion.

WHAT LIONS LOOK LIKE

Male lions weigh about 350 to 400 pounds (158 to 181 kilograms) and are just under 9 feet (2.7 meters) long. Females weigh about 300 pounds (136 kilograms) and are about 8 feet (2.4 meters) long.

Most large female and male cats look alike. But male and female lions do not look the same. Males have thick manes of hair. They also have tufts of hair on their elbows, chests, and shoulders. Females do not have this extra hair.

Lions are yellow brown. This color is very like the grass and brown earth on the African plains where they live. This means lions are well **camouflaged**.

A male African lion looks for a shady place to nap.

WHERE LIONS LIVE

Today lions live mostly in Africa. They can be found in the countries of Kenya, Tanzania, Uganda, Zambia, Botswana, South Africa, and Angola. A few lions still live in Asia, in northwest India. But that number gets smaller every year.

Lions like grassy plains and open woodlands where there are not many trees. These places are known as the lion's **habitat**.

A young lion finishes its meal of wildebeest.

Part of a pride of African lions rests in the shade of a lone tree.

A young lion still shows some of the spots it had as a cub.

HOW LIONS LIVE

Lions move slowly and like to rest. Still, they can swim, climb trees, and jump nearly 12 feet (3.6 meters) in one leap. They can run as fast as 35 miles an hour (56 kilometers an hour).

Most cats like to live alone. But lions enjoy company. They live together in groups known as **prides**. Lions like to hunt together. The male lions defend their **territory** against other lions.

After having food and water, these lions will look for a place to nap.

LION CUBS

Lion cubs are born about 3-1/2 months after the male and female have mated. There are usually two to four cubs born. They are born blind but can begin to see after about a week.

The mother lioness protects the newborn cubs. Young lions depend on their mother for food until they are a year and a half old.

Lion cubs are easy prey for other animals.

PREDATOR AND PREY

Lions often hunt during the day. The female lion does most of the hunting. The lions usually find their **prey** by sight. The lion moves slowly and quietly, **stalking** its prey. Then, it charges. The lion kills with its teeth and claws.

The lion is the strongest **predator** in its habitat. Lions kill antelopes, zebras, ostriches, and many other animals. They also **scavenge**. This means they eat animals that have been killed by others.

This wildebeest will provide food for the lion's family.

LIONS AND PEOPLE

Lions have always interested humans. Thousands of years ago, the ancient Egyptians kept lions. The Romans used lions to fight against humans in their arenas. A former king of England was known as Richard the Lion-Hearted.

More recently, lions have been big attractions in zoos and circuses.

Perched on a termite mound, these lions are safe in an African national park.

THE FUTURE OF LIONS

Lions in India may number about 300. Even in Africa there are probably only about 200,000 lions. Lions disappear because their habitats are disappearing. In Africa much of the plains are being turned into farmlands. As crops increase, the number of lions will continue to decrease.

Some lions are protected in African wildlife parks, but this care will not save many lions.

GLOSSARY

camouflaged (CAM oh flajd) — hidden from sight because an animal's color matches its surroundings

carnivore (CAR nuh vor) — an animal that is mostly or all a meat eater

felines (FEE linz) — any of the cats

habitat (HAB uh tat) — the area in which an animal lives

predator (PRED uh tor) — an animal that kills another animal for food

prey (PRAY) — an animal that is hunted for food by another animal

prides (PRYDZ) — groups of lions with family ties

scavenge (SCAV enj) — to feed on the remains of animals not killed by the feeder

species (SPEE seez) — one certain kind, within a group of closely related animals

stalking (STOCK ing) — hunting by slowly and quietly moving toward the victim

territory (TARE uh TOR ee) — a home area defended by certain animals that live within it

INDEX

Further Reading

Lee, Sandra. *Lions*. Child's World, 2001
Denis-Huot, Christine. *Lions, King of the Beasts*. Charlesbridge, 2000

Websites To Visit

http://www.lionresearch.org/
http://www.nationalgeographic.com/kids/creature_feature/0109/

About The Author

Jason Cooper has written several children's books about a variety of topics for Rourke Publishing, including recent series *China Discovery* and *American Landmarks.* Cooper travels widely to gather information for his books. Two of his favorite travel destinations are Alaska and the Far East.